Love's
EPITAPH

PRATYAY CHAUDHURI

 Scribe

Love's Epitaph

Publisher: Inkscribe Media Pvt. Ltd

ISBN Number: 978-1-966421-40-5

"We don't read and write poetry because it's cute. We read and write poetry because we are members of the human race."

-N.H Kleinbaum, *Dead Poets Society.*

Contents

.

Foreword

The very essence of poetry and in fact, life itself remains soulfully ingrained in the words that we leave unspoken everyday. When I first picked up the pen, I did it to create a space for myself. The emotions that the world might deem as too much always found a way into my notepads and eventually into the hearts of my friends and family. The love that my work has received from the few people in my life who value poetry for what it truly is, has prompted me to compile my works for a wider audience.

When you do decide to pick up this book, I hope you find relatability in the words that you experience, and appreciate the depths of catharsis that some unexpressed emotions can provide.

My greatest satisfaction as a poet would be in you reading the book aloud in your room, living every line, allowing it to hold your hand, maybe even letting it lend its shoulder for you to cry upon through all this hurt.

I sincerely hope you can bury all of the pain in this grave. The epitaph is ready.

Epitaph

The mania of memories are at loose again,

They run amok amidst the ruins of a castle I built by the lake.

No, not the one where the poets came to die,

Not the one where the world stopped and silently watched them cry.

A lake where the sky melted with all its stars,

As Vincent painted it on his canvas, just to be shunned,

As the blood dripped from his severed ear,

He must have hysterically laughed at how far one had to go,

Seeking love as an outcast.

The soothing silence of those blackbirds,

Pierces my soul tonight,

With arrows I had sent out years ago,

Hoping for them to reach the other side of this lake.

I send stones now, skipping on the surface,

Rippling it with waves that will not reach you tonight,

A lover by fate, denied of love by destiny,

Hallucinating of a castle I built in your name,

And cursing the day it came crashing down,

Your name still remains.

Not drowning in that lake like I was,

Just washed by a solitary tear,

That was our love's epitaph.

Fireflies

Till death do us part, we vowed,

And in a grave we turned up,

Writing epitaphs for each other,

Finding stones hard enough to combat time.

The ones who come with flowers every morning,

Probably burn as they pass our names,

The dust-laden sepulchre, a testament to the neglect,

A neglect only the outer world sees.

Inside amidst the worms and earth,

There is a glow that lights up our bones,

A glow that keeps entangled our useless frames,

As we lie facing each other.

What do the fireflies know of our love?

I ask them, as they magnanimously light up our stones
at nightfall,

Are they the ones who kept us company as we kissed at midnight?

Did they bathe us with a spiritual luminosity as our bodies blended into each other?

Witnesses, they were of me worshipping every curve, every scar on your flesh.

Flesh.

Overly glorified for something that melts, and is devoured by lowly invertebrates.

Bones.

Horrid artefacts of our mortality, even they aren't eternal.

Eternal is what I have for you and what you have for me,

Eternal is the void that we left on this mortal world that lives above the soil,

Eternal are the missiles that now light up the skies,

And yes, eternal are those fireflies.

Chisel

Let the north wind that blows into your room,

Ruffling those satin curtains guide you.

If you walk along the shivering frenzy,

You'll find yourself on the south wing staircase.

The staircase will lead you to me,

Stone cold, you'll see me stand, perhaps frozen in time.

If you touch me tonight,

You'll be greeted by the sheen on my ivory white skin,

Bathed by a pétillant moonlight.

The chisel that shaped me,

The rasps that added enticing beauty to my body,

Didn't refrain from making it known what I was made for.

The nudity that clothes my bust,

The frail peace of cloth reluctantly sculpted around my waist,

Leaving me vulnerable to the wild winds and salacious eyes,

Pierce my skin every time I think of myself as human.

If you've come to drink in my body,

I'm powerless to stop you.

But while you're here, do hear me play the violin I pray,

For I'll weave a tune from the chill of these hills,

A tune that'll crescendo into tears of womanhood.

In a strange satire, and a cruel fable,

A rock feels the plight of a woman,

But you do not.

You make me wonder why those gazes are so lustful, touches wanton,

Then I remember–

The chisel made me a woman, not human.

Fault

So, whose fault is it?

Whose fault is it that I still crave for your presence in a crowded room,

That I still feel the emptiness in my voice when I hear myself talk,

That my shoulders crave for your hair to effortlessly fall on them, again?

I wonder how your view was when our dreams got engulfed in that raging fire,

A fire sparked with pebbles of insecurity and distrust,

Slowly accumulating, brushing silently against each other,

The flame taking hold of the twigs of hope that we had collected together.

I wonder who the villain is in your story.

The villain who couldn't stand what we had, and when it finally had enough,

Ripped us into shreds.

The villain in your story is a lover of silence,

Who used to bask in the simple pleasure of your presence,

Would keep looking at your pictures when things got dark,

And would give up anything just to touch your skin.

As the cold January air assaults my temples,

I lean against the glass just to feel the cold of this season,

The reptilian gloss of my blazer satin,

A shimmering daub of worry on my body,

Makes me wonder,

Whose fault is it?

Mistletoe

The mistletoe ruffles with a snowy breeze that comes in.

Haven't lit up the tree yet,

Still waiting for it to be dark enough,

Still waiting for it to be cold enough in my room.

The thermostat malfunctioned last night,

Sat with my limbs huddled together in a blanket,

Trying to fight off the cold.

It was probably on a night like this that Frost had wandered off into the woods,

If I wanted to, I'd have to make do with concrete though,

The solitude elusive, betrayal looming large in the faces around me.

The ones who'd be lucky enough to stay up all night, trying to catch a glimpse of Father Christmas,

Don't know that the mistletoe on their Christmas trees is poisonous.

Wait, I wasn't supposed to break that to you.

You waited all year for a night of warmth and family only to be greeted by someone as cold as me.

I'm sorry for the cold in my room tonight,

And you, of all people know that I'd never put up the lights.

I think you should probably head out to a room full of lights and people,

A place where the carols and aroma of a roast fill the void of a cribbed heart.

Oh, whilst you head out, turn the porch light off,

And wish them on my wretched behalf,

A Merry Christmas…

Mute

I woke up to discover that I had lost my voice.

A trusted companion, a friend on most days, my voice had finally betrayed me.

There was this overwhelming urge to shout,

And yet every decibel was muffled,

Every scream blocked out.

What felt worse however,

Was that people didn't notice,

Stranded with a million thoughts, I was,

And yet, nothing was amiss.

The air hung heavy around me,

People at work continued to chatter,

And for the first time in my life,

It felt like I didn't matter.

I started preparing to live life this way,

A plethora of gesture and expressions,

Diphthongs and alliterations things of the past,

And yet, it didn't make a difference,

That I was dying of a heavy heart.

Desperation was at its peak,

As I searched frantically for my voice,

Bestial notes were all I had to offer,

Every sinew taut, larynx stiffer.

But a lesson I did learn,

I lacked voice that day, and they concern.

Shadow

It was a similar night,

A darkness, dense, grotesque, closed in on me.

I vied for an escape,

Oblivious to what I wanted to escape from.

I searched for a hand to hold,

As my fingers trembled,

I sought a shoulder to rest my head on,

As my temples throbbed with a dull ache.

A distant light filtered in through my frosted window,

A shadow loomed of my lonesome past,

That craved for a cradle of words,

A listener to my musings,

Or did I just miss what it used to be?

I pulled my blanket up,

To cover up my insecurities, my worries,

All those things I feared would push you away.

Now I don't have to fear that though,

I don't stay awake to talk to that shadow,

For my worries won't sting you anymore.

So I throw the blanket aside,

Laying myself bare to a shadow.

Grief is that shadow,

Grief is all that love that has no place to go...

Empathy's Curse

The chair invites me into an alluring darkness,

Seeped in memories of the time we spent,

From a distance so far,

That our fingers wouldn't touch anymore.

The vapours that cloud around your shower,

Mist up the mirror you see yourself in,

As you search for your true self.

Do the drops of water warm on your skin,

Sting however, with a sharp cold?

Does your bath fill up with blood that you spilled,

When you slit the throat of what we had?

The chair in my room reminisces of the urge in my voice,

Searching desperately for what caused that silence within you,

Tears that blurred my vision when I found out,

That I'd lost the way around your mind.

You come out of the shower,

Your hair dripping wet, brown, or was it a vengeful crimson?

Crimson is the dress you'll slip into tonight,

Flashing bulbs, sequins of light,

High voices, a drunken fight,

Of souls searching for an easy escape.

I sit still on that chair,

Feeling every molecule on its surface,

Every interlocking in its lattice,

Still shaking with what broke us,

A fever of differences,

Empathy's curse.

Curtains

Draw the curtains, let the light in,

How many more days will you spend,

Sleeping in?

Let the light wash over your skin,

Gooseflesh from the terrors you let in.

Go ahead, open that window,

Let the breeze ruffle your unkempt hair,

Let the smoke make you cough,

Let the horns roughen you up.

The honey drizzles in concentric swirls on your pancakes,

Lick that last drop from the spoon,

Drink it from the jar, I don't mind.

A poet died last night,

Let's toast to her plight.

Run a bath, watch yourself wait for it in the mirror,

Throw in a few words in praise of what you see,

Get in, stay a little longer,

Let your skin feel the warmth no one has ever made you feel.

Get out, put on some clothes,

And shades of your choice, important that bit.

Hurry along, you're late for work.

Forget work.

You go there everyday.

You were getting ready for something else today.

A date with yourself maybe,

Don't sweat it, you can stay home today,

You might not be all that wealthy,

You can afford to breathe today,

And maybe resurrect that poet that died yesterday...

Voice

The voice that drifts into my room,

Reminds of the glacé you bound me with.

An ethereal weave of notes, you grace everyone with,

Play on my gramophone tonight.

Not too unfamiliar with the damp of this apartment,

Entwined in a cherry wine fragrance that you left,

All those years ago,

Your voice soothes every fibre of this insomniac.

Blasé as my taste is in music,

It still waits for your voice to play.

The record that never stops playing in this house,

The stylus that blunts itself from the relentless scratching on the vinyl,

Much like my cries felt the night you left,

Still holds on for my sinful pleasure.

The void that slowly builds every night,

Enters my bloodstream, as you crack open my skin,

With your blissful crescendo.

Sweet nights they were when we melted into each other,

Only bitter memories now as I am, but a frozen block of ice,

Still manoeuvring through faked laughs,

And suppressed cries…

Letter

and if that day ever chances upon our porch,

that sees you leave,

I'd stop you in front of that gate, and ask you to stay.

I'd get down on my knees, and beg, even,

to not let this little home I have, crumble into nothingness.

I'd pluck out that lily from the kitchen garden and gift it you,

just like you did years ago,

and if you still insist, I'd let you go,

for I can't bear to see you in captivity.

the bird of freedom you are,

it will perhaps make me smile for one last time,

you spreading your wings,

a million skies in your eyes,

just like your gentle hands on my face…

but I'd write you one letter every month,

addressed to the skies, for I hope that's where you'll soar,

wishing upon you, the best, of luck, love and everything there is to wish for.

you will be in another set of arms,

with a soul that loves you more than me perhaps,

if it indeed is possible to love you more than me.

write back to me back that day.

the day you think my love was exceeded by another soul,

come to my front yard and throw that letter on my face.

you'll see me burn, with that letter, and an undying desire for your lips on mine,

for one last time…

Scottish Rain

The church spires congregate in an eerie silence this evening.

A grave hymn diffusing through the cold Scottish air,

Greets your ears with the coldness of steel...

The clock tower resonates with seven bells,

The last one leaving a shrill after-tone that had a strange authority,

Over me, you and all of the wretched inhabitants of this stone-cold city.

I remember walks we had on the gravel path,

Leading up to that tiny cottage we called our own...

A miraculous turn of the hour-glass sees me walk alone on that very same path,

Towards my home, or my doom perhaps.

The December chill that threatens to freeze me to my death,

And yet, I do nothing to fight it off.

The Lochs that embraced us with their baltic touch,

Will probably freeze my lonely self, dreich as I am,

In another bleak landscape.

The warmth of your hands on my skin,

The soft brush of your lips against mine,

Reminds me of warmer days that we'd seen together.

The Macallan burns on its way down, reminding me
of the void that exists,

In this heart, in this city, in my home.

Here I am, waiting for you to turn up again,

All drenched in this fatal Scottish rain…

Starry Night

A blanket of stars that greeted them that night,

Was all the light there was.

A city brought to a halt by a power cut,

Something so catastrophic to work, life and economy,

And yet their eyes twinkled into that night so dreamy,

The two wrapped in a shawl watched on,

Spotting Cancer, Aries and Aquila,

Hairs messy from the sweet breeze that enticed their senses,

A heightened response perhaps to the sudden assault of darkness,

On their blurry lenses.

With her head gracefully perched on his shoulder,

His hands embracing her like she was his only buoy in this rude wild world,

The two feared of a bond that was forming between them.

An inevitable, driven by the utter force of the love there was,

Made the two of them surrender to their fate that night.

They feared attachment all along for the heart-wreck that usually followed,

And chased them all their lives.

And yet, here they were on a starry, starry night,

Feeling for the strings that tied them,

Only this time, ever so tight!

Phiran

Unpacking the phiran that you gifted,

Was the happiest moment of last winter.

It somehow is the happiest moment of this one too.

Hand-wrapped in mauve art-paper,

Graced with a tulip tucked into the silk ribbon,

It had the rustic enchantment of those letters we sent each other,

Only a million times sweeter than my inept words,

Almost at par with your blissful shayari,

As the garment was slowly stripped off its package,

An age-old smell of that treasured pashmina greeted my nostrils.

The warmth of the wool was a welcome reprieve from the cold of your absence,

Those long sleeves, with its immaculate embroidery,

Wrapped me up in an embrace,

The kind only you had mastered.

The poignance of the gift you sent from your fabled paradise,

Kept me company for the whole of this winter.

Every thread haunting me with the sweetness of your breath,

Every loose strand reminding me of distance,

I know it's cold there,

Without your letters and tulips, my city gets colder by the day,

As if in an insane race to match the coldness of your heart,

Or the race to your arms, I want to run,

But miles away, I comfort myself in your phiran…

Kaftaan

(A reply to Phiran)

Unpacking the kaftaan you gifted was the happiest memory of that winter.

But it isn't the happiest memory of this one.

In a careless grace of its inconspicuous attraction,

It arrived from your land of promise.

The land where the river next to my cottage flows,

Probably carrying with it drops of blood from my bleeding heart everyday.

A heart that bleeds today, perhaps had it's first gash from neglect,

A deprivation of assiduity, a deprivation of love.

It bleeds days into nights, for it lacked the nurture that a wound needs to heal,

The cries of desperate eyes for a heedless vanity,

Still echoes in my valley,

You were always an expert at concealment,

The scarlet fabric of the kaftaan adept at hiding the blood on my chest,

The coldness of the fabric that hugged me through nights I wanted your warmth,

The loose ends of those threads caressing the scars you drew on my body,

The grosgrain ribbon slowly strangling every bit of my shameless hope.

The kaftaan burns today in my fireplace.

The flames go up in celebration of an end,

And my heart freezes to congeal the blood.

Door

Banging on your door will be a tired fist,

Slowly opening up from the reactionary blows,

A spatter of blood from the knuckles,

That lost skin from the impact they made,

Impact of desperation, impact of despair,

An eerie silence that it was greeted with,

Resonates throughout the corridor.

Not a pinhole remains on the mahogany,

Knocked shut with force,

A force that love tries to counter,

But fails to bore...

You'll hear a cry from behind that door,

Of a voice weakened with fatigue,

A voice that cried for your help,

A voice from in too deep.

Time ripens, as the clock strikes past the dark hour,

And the voice silences itself.

But you hear a whisper,

A smile that hid many a tear.

A smile that still wants to hear you talk,

Eyes that want to see you for just once.

The blood remains on your door,

Your silence was the lance,

Come tomorrow you'll open that door,

And you'll have blood on your hands…

Hotel

A blurred view of this valley,

Through the pellucid glass of a dingy hotel room,

Is what greeted me that morning.

An eclectic canvas of a million emotions,

The last page of a hundred relationships,

The footnote of many a eulogy,

The four walls of this room, has perhaps seen it all.

It has shaped lives, it has destroyed them,

It has kindled many a spirit, doused some,

With an ice-cold sprinkling from the river that flows
past it.

A gagging sweetness overhangs the room,

Almost overdoing its part of masking the smell of
pasts.

Or is it your scent that greets my nostrils?

A grating static from the television set finds its way to
my ears,

A sound so familiar, yet so foreign,

Pulling me down into a bottomless pit that is this bed today.

A bed with its memories of mortal vices,

A bed that witnessed the passion of tormented souls,

Slowly suffers in silence, the burns of many a cigar foot.

The television static gives way to framed moments of darkness,

And the darkness, replaced by the outline of a face,

A face I hold dear, a face I called life one day.

My eyes opened with a gasp for breath.

My senses had got it fatally wrong,

You weren't beside me,

But the night was still young.

Breakup

'Breakup' is a heavy word.

We didn't have it.

I don't cry in the backseat of my car to your favourite song,

Reminiscing of you beside me.

Why would I?

I never had you there.

I never taste your lipstick when I lick your favourite ice cream.

Why would I?

We never shared a cone.

I didn't picture your face when we were told to embrace our loved ones at a concert.

Why would I?

I didn't love you.

Or for the world, I didn't.

I don't stay up till 2am, throwing paper planes of thoughts,

At a wall of 'what if's.

Why would I?

I never imagined a night with you.

Too big to fit into plans,

Too quiet to ever sustain a conversation,

Adept at hiding my regrets about that,

I kept walking away.

Perhaps, I did walk away a little too far from your life.

Perhaps, it was for the better that we weren't together,

For then I would have to weigh the pain of losing you against the pain of never having you.

As I said, 'breakup' is a heavy word,

Thank heavens, we don't carry it.

Do we find love?

"Do we find love?"

My younger self asks me with a glimmer of eagerness,

It's only halfway into an overcast night,

And I don't find in me, the heart to disappoint him.

How do I break it to him?

How do I tell him her name?

How do I tell him of the scars that those days of waiting left on my body?

How do I tell him how I felt oceans and yet drowned in the shallows of it all?

The shallows of a heart-wrenching call that went unanswered,

How do I tell him that I found myself-

Ankle-deep in rain,

Waist-deep in love,

And neck-deep in debt,

A debt to myself.

A debt that would slowly drive me into ruination,

Had I not grasped the helm with profound desperation one day…

I had saved the ship,

I had saved it with love,

For me, for hope, and for a heart that never ceases to love with everything.

I looked into his eyes and answered,

"Yes, we do…"

Harmless Lie

The gramophone plays a stifled tune tonight.

As the needle scrapes out those notes from that record,

My gaze fixated on the skylight,

Searches for peace amidst the darkness of an uneventful night.

Lost in the all-consuming conundrum of moral ambiguity,

I search for answers I didn't get from you.

Sleepless nights spent waiting for an answer,

Countless days spent waiting for a rendezvous,

That never happened.

The moon changed phases,

The tides turned and yet some stains never seeped out of my shirt.

The fragrance of that cologne I saved for our date,

Still lingers on my shirt and torments my olfaction,

With a gagging sweetness every time I open my wardrobe...

On nights like these, I imagine a reality,

A reality where we would look at the same sky,

Fingers intertwined, your hair caressing my face,

Something only your sight could do till then,

A wilful conspiracy of our timelines,

Or by a ruthless whim, we won't meet again.

And yet after all this time, I only need the universe to tell me,

That it was all a lie, an outrageous, heart-shattering and yet,

A harmless lie...

Dusk by the river

As the chimney-smoke swirled it's way up into the dusk,

The town shrouded itself in a winter haze.

A grey haze, a muffled symphony of a tiring population,

Returning home on ferries.

This is exactly why I hated the ghats.

A thousand places in this town and yet,

Gloom chooses this very place to dive into the river.

You're wondering why I'm sitting by the river,

At this particularly depressing hour, lost in my head.

Well, I was persuaded.

"Let's sit by the river and talk life.", this is exactly what she said.

How could I say 'no'?

Sipping tea out of two earthen pots of innocence,

We talked 'life'.

No, not the chewed-out pulp of existential paradox we called 'life'.

'Life' to me had a different meaning when she was around.

'Life' existed in those deep-set russet eyes, that peeked over those spectacles sometimes,

'Life' existed in those delicate feet, in that little skin visible through a pair of Birkenstocks,

'Life' existed in her smile and the rim of that kulhad her lipstick had graced,

'Life' existed in her,

And everything around was dead,

Waiting to be resurrected by her shoulder, resting my head...

Saigon

Waiting for the call lines to form,

I tapped my feet on the wooden floor.

The unconscious rhythm that formed within the booth,

Rings in my ears still.

Oh, how I hoped those notes reached overseas,

Notwithstanding the hindrance it'd pose to our conversation,

I still wanted you to sense a part of me,

That existed beyond my voice.

I wanted you to remember how it used to be,

When we walked the streets of this Oriental dream,

The smell of spring rolls and bành mí,

The sights of Ao dai and lacquered pottery,

Of red banners and a liberation street.

You knew my country as well as I did,

Every nook and cranny of Saigon,

That smelled of a pot of pho kept too long,

As we spent hours talking in that book street.

I didn't see you in the star-spangled banners that your friends carry today,

A part of me that still craves,

For what we were before I'd seen you that fateful day.

I fell deep into those dark blue eyes,

In how you held my body through my cries,

How our silhouettes blended every night.

And now that the bombing has stopped,

I cry of how I misinterpreted the blue in those eyes.

The blue that was meant to background the Stars and Stripes,

Whose only true intent was to wipe out the red,

My nation, my heart bleeds, for it was wasted to feed your nation's greed,

And I to your passion.

And yet, the red flies high over our street,

Wish you could see it through the phone lines,

Of how the north and south meet.

December Rains

You know, it rained this December.

Who would have thought, right?

A cold month, with the warmest afternoon sun,

A month of memories and cakes,

A month of developing those retakes,

Of every picture you made me click again,

Just because your feet missed the frame...

Imagine all of that, with a splash of water on it!

As the sepia of the evenings faded into a dull grey,

The smell of your sweater was suddenly stronger than my coffee,

Your hair nestled like a queen on my hoodie,

Like you still are, a little deeper down, in my heart.

As the cake gags me with its sweetness,

A faint silhouette of a that nude you wore on your lips,

Still lingers on my cheeks.

A bead from that bracelet you wore to our first date stays with me,

I feel it in my pocket, as close as your smile when I hid it,

While you were putting it together.

Wish my heart stopped skipping a beat at every mention of you,

But the rain flooded those wishes, in a slush of nostalgia.

As I threw my last letter into the warm fireplace hue,

The placid embers made me wonder,

"Was the rain here too?"

Chenab

Night fell, the moon glowed in its ethereal radiance,

It was a night for lovers,

It was a night for serenity,

Only the might of a river separated them.

A river so beautiful by the day,

A roaring stream of fury by night,

She didn't need to worry though,

Her trusted vessel was hers to row.

The vessel touched the immense river,

Ready for its width,

But soon started melting away, into the night.

The melting pot dragged her down, into the freezing Chenab,

All those little dreams, crashing into the pebbles,

As the river gorged its way through, it carried with it two hearts,

Two hearts full of hope,

Hope for a future,

Hope for the other's company,

All stifled out.

But can hope be stifled out?

The river carried them away to a heaven of their own,

A heaven where all differences perished,

And only their love shone....

Monsoon Rant

They always romanticise the rain,

I don't know what they see in those drops,

Blurred glasses, clogged roads,

Stranded people searching souls.

They'll label me unromantic,

They are probably right.

No one expects a poet to not love the rain,

To not write words that worship it's serenity,

To not paint pictures as fluidly vivid as the monsoon,

I try, I try to please them.

I search for phrases that can do justice to this heavenly gift,

I look out my car window to see kids dancing in the mud,

I see a mother hurriedly get her kid into a raincoat,

I see a couple, their bodies in a half embrace trying to fit into one umbrella.

Three different scenes and yet they hit me the same,

The pain of a thousand shrapnels falling on me,

I stare at the drops on the window, with stunned silence,

You see, I didn't romanticise the rain for I never found joy in it.

I'll write something once those drops make me happy,

For now, you should go back to singing songs to the rain,

And let me learn how to romanticise pain...

Date

I find my finger slowly tracing something on the window pane,

An index finger, euphorically shivers as the vapours part,

Paving the way for my skin to trace something beautiful…

Halfway through, the first glance of my misty creation hits me.

Two numbers, signifying the day,

Two more numbers later, a part of you shaped,

In those droplets, in the form your birthday…

The blurred view that my window offers tonight,

Complemented fittingly by my blurred vision,

Doesn't hide your silhouette playing on the grass,

Your voice, your smell diffusing through the cold night air,

Like a distant theatricality playing out on the horizon.

You're in someone else's arms tonight,

As I trace some numbers again,

The vapours part to shelter another date,

Only this time my fingers tremble in pain,

For that date, comes back to haunt me in my sleep,

A day when your silhouette vanished from my window,

A day when that dream I painted was washed off the canvas,

In a tepid, relentless rain that kept kissing the grass...

Selling poems

I have a dream of selling poems for a living.

My mother says I'll go broke,

She's probably right.

No one cares for poetry these days.

All they want to do is to glorify your pain, after you die.

Don't believe me?

Ask Van Gogh or Rumi.

Poems can be dry,

And yet there are some,

Which will make you cry...

I'll be there at a boulevard on the hills,

Sheets of paper, a heart and some ink,

I promise I won't write sad stuff,

I'll write of the mountains, meadows and streams,

I'll write of clouds and a shepherd's peace,

I know I won't sell even one of my poems.

Who wants to read what they can see?

I'll put down my quill, and take out that piece of fragrant paper.

A paper that bore the brunt of my youthful insanity,

If you happen to stroll by,

Will you buy that piece?

I'll charge your blissful smile,

And hope you'll read what you didn't see...

Wishes

I could never stop my pen from snitching on my heart.

I've written umpteen poems about you, some sweet, some bitter,

A few of those that left butterflies,

Others, just chords of an incoherent guitar.

I guess our time has run it's course,

You have no idea though,

Of my nights of incessant remorse,

Of those moments when my heart held you close.

I remember that day when I saw tears in your eyes,

It felt like cold steel on my frigid heart,

Stabbing through ice.

I wanted to comfort you, wipe away those tears,

But I had no right to,

Always swept away by a thousand fears...

Now that our time has run it's course,

I'll spool out those memories,

Memories of our conversations, an occasional wave,

Or a smile here and there.

I'll frame them up and keep them near,

Wishing another heart loves you dear,

And never again in a million years,

Lets you shed another tear.

Thread

It's one of those nights again.

I can't sleep,

And I'm petrified to check the time because I know it's late.

I'm tossing and turning on my bed, trying to make peace with myself,

Trying to sing lullabies to the vicious cycles of thoughts clouding my head.

They never really warn you,

They don't tell you how despairing a wait for a text can be,

They don't tell you how heartbreaking a smile can be.

They don't teach you how to hide pain behind your smile,

But if you don't, they call you fragile.

Sometimes my subconscious shows me a thread connecting our hearts,

Lately I've seen it turn frail,

Fading away into the darkness,

I know it'll tear soon,

A frail thread can only hold so much…

When it tears though,

Can I keep a piece of that thread with me?

To see me through those sleepless nights,

To give peace amidst those tumultuous tides,

I'll need that thread…

Don't worry though, I'm moving on,

But I still don't know what's more painful–

Letting go or holding on?

Coping

What do you do on those nights?

When memories stomp your courtyard in a chaotic cavalcade,

When whiskey burns your throat,

And denies you even a moment's shade?

I'll tell you what I do.

Along the shores, I walk, humming our favourite songs,

Or watch the cotton candies sell,

Some nights, I just lie down on the grass,

Hozier playing on the speaker,

I find myself in a trance.

A worshipping lover in his near-ethereal voice,

Asks me, "Was I not enough?"

Then there are days, when I am a different man.

Drinking in the atrocities of this unforgiving town,

Orchestrating a mayhem,

Where the trumpets were never in tune.

The wreck that I find myself in on those days,

Ends by sundown.

I find myself surrounded by drapes of burgundy,

Drowning in the seductive Bloody Mary,

Thinking how you were once a certainty,

Now not even a maybe…

That song

I don't know what happened,

But these days, I can't listen to that song anymore.

As soon as I play it, the lyrics run over me with pangs of anguish,

The melody sharp as a thousand blades.

The song spoke of monsoon, the salt air brushing my hair,

Like the thought of you did sometimes.

The rust on your door was something real,

Somewhat close to my chest.

Someone asked me why I entangle this song with you,

A song of emptiness, a song of wishes that didn't come true,

I couldn't answer then.

Maybe, it spoke of how far I'd go,

How long I'll wait,

How much I'd give up,

Just for you…

Today, as I stand upon the ruins of that song,

I know the answer.

You know, it had to be that song.

A song of broken strings,

A song where wanting had to be enough,

At least for me, it was enough…

Next Fall

Today I saw you get down the stairs.

Our eyes probably met for a flirting second. Or maybe it didn't.

To you, I am still just another guy,

An unnecessary passer-by,

In the realms of my subconscious,

I am not this shy.

I have called you my love,

As we gazed into the night sky,

In our dreams, we can conjure up anything we want,

A lovely home, a lavish porch,

Or a terrace with a view,

But in my dreams, there is this diffuse ether,

And only you.

I sometimes laugh at the helplessness of my love,

I am scared to call it 'love' in front of friends,

They might call it naïveté

But I wish they had my lens.

I have waited way too long,

I guess one day I'll just stop.

But if I can't,

Let's just meet next fall.

Hand to hold

You'll be sitting in the theatre,

Watching that young boy propose to his lover,

Or by the lake, counting those swans swimming home for sundown,

Or just stargaze your evenings away,

In the clutches of this blasphemous city…

In all those moments, you'll search for a hand to hold.

There'll be days when things would be bleak,

Life would feel like a noir,

Caffeine wouldn't give you the shot you need.

Your reverie would be broken every now and then,

By the screeching of a relentless chainsaw your life would be then.

Then my love, you'd search for a hand to hold.

A soft brush of skin,

And then slowly you'll intertwine your fingers around his,

Just when the actors kiss,

Just when the swans reach home,

Just when you spot Orion on the sky,

You'd squeeze that hand.

The sweet serendipity of it will be shattered,

As if by a counter-spell,

Or just the ephemeral pain of separation,

Remember then, my love,

Not all hands you squeeze, will squeeze yours back.

A Different Wedding

Smiling guests, exquisite orchids, me in the best tux I have.

I stand at the altar looking down the aisle,

You walk towards me, flanked by flower girls and that elixir of a smile.

I snap my fingers and my best man does the needful,

Seconds later, we hear 'Love Story' playing in the background.

I get down on my knees and offer you the wedding ring,

You start singing, "Romeo take me…"

That's the wedding I had always imagined. That's what I thought our dream day would be like before I drove into the bridge rails with a sickening crunch on a foggy winter evening. It was nine months before I came out of the hospital, with a leg lost and partially blind, but most importantly with a heart shattered. They said I was lucky to even be alive. I thanked my stars but also cursed them for being so cruel.

Fast forward five more months and I find myself in the patio.

Smiling guests, exquisite orchids, me in the best tux I have?

None of that.

I find myself in a wheelchair instead.

You sit right across from me.

What remains the same is that elixir of a smile through my failing eyes.

You snap your fingers, and the speakers boom,

You start singing, "I like shiny things but I'd marry you with paper rings"

Paper plane

Always wondered what this town would look like,

From the tallest tank I knew,

For we don't have skyscrapers,

Not even a church spire comes into view.

Shimmering below are a few hundred houses,

Each keeping to their own.

One of those houses, I know, belong to you.

I don't know which one, though.

I'm here tonight to write a poem,

A poem about you…

I know others do a far better job than me,

Painting you on canvases and city murals,

They look beautiful, but none even close to you…

This is perhaps because you were never meant to be drawn,

Pens and brushes can never do you justice,

So I try with thoughts,

One day, you'll probably come across this piece of paper,

Or maybe you're reading it right now.

I hope you sense how shallow this monologue is,

Just send me a few words, somehow…

I'm folding this paper up into a plane,

I'll throw it into the night sky,

Hoping that it pierces the darkness like a torch,

And daintily lands on your porch.

I know it won't reach that far,

But I made a wish,

Ask that shooting star….

Window to my skies

The first time you looked at me,

I found myself in a trance.

There was peace in those eyes,

And the turmoil of a thousand storms.

My heart has always belonged to the mountains,

An admirer of the valleys and the serene rivers that flow,

A manifested reality of dreams that'd make my eyes glow...

You'd think I fall for beauty,

One that entraps the eyes.

You'd be mistaken though.

With all the chaotic scars that inhabit my heart,

I fell for the peace in you...

You remain as unshakable as those mountains,

Me, a mere tourist taking in the landscape,

Didn't know when that landscape became a portrait,

A portrait of your eyes,

But those eyes always looked away.

Look away,

May the World know the true worth of those pearls.

I never had the right to look into those eyes,

But they were the window to my skies...

Sticky Note

The spaghetti cools on the table,

The fragrance of the coffee beans you crushed still lingers,

Like a bitter aftertaste of what could've been.

I look out the window.

No, it isn't cloudy like those other poets would make you believe,

The birds sing, the children play, the cars zoom past on the streets,

A cacophony soothing enough for your playlist,

It doesn't soothe me anymore.

Nothing does, really.

The merciless nonchalance of this brutal world strangles me…

I look up from my plate,

I see the note you left on the refrigerator door,

I try looking away but not before my vision blurs.

I lie my weary self down on the couch,

Yes, this is where I sleep now,

Or at least I make a feeble attempt at it.

No, don't ask me why I don't go up to the bedroom,

Gnarly memories of many a sweet night we spent there,

Wind me up in shackles of armoured metal.

I steal another furtive glance at that sticky note,

It says, "We need to talk."

I cry out in agreement, "Yes, we do!"

But then I remember that the door's shut!

You left with a note on the refrigerator door,

And a blemish on my heart…

Stage

Just so you know, I don't belong here,

Not on stage, not amongst the audience…

The senseless hollering they call music these days suffocate me,

The flash lights blind me,

It feels like drowning in an ocean of happy souls,

And I don't know how to drink it…

You ask me why

I'm here.

He who remains lost in the blissful solitude of his room,

He who spends days wound up in his mind,

He shouldn't be here, should he?

Well, I'm here for a reason.

I'm here to watch you get on stage,

I'm here to watch you set it on fire,

I'm here to drink your voice and raise a toast with it...

A toast to the one who gifts me the tranquillity of a thousand valleys,

A toast to the one whose smile transcends the ethereal.

You get up on stage.

And like every other time, you do justice to your name,

Lost amidst a thousand cheers and flashing lights,

I smile.

I know I don't have the right to be proud of you.

I know I don't have the right to silence them all and shout out your name into the microphone,

But a part of me wants to do all that,

The part of me that I have given to you,

You don't know but it'll always be yours.

By the way,

Did you see me wave?

Teddy

The day had worn her down,

It was cold and gloomy,

The world looked at her with a frown.

She always wanted to run away,

Away from those judging eyes,

Away from those scarring lies,

Oh, they hurt her so much.

But she was here to fight,

So with clenched jaws and closed fists,

Bravely did she take those hits.

But in the end, all she craved for,

Was her father's hand on her brow,

Or her mother's kiss...

She wished to wrestle her little brother again,

And wrap him up in her arms,

She wished to hear her granny's laugh,

Or wear that sweater she weaved.

Miles away from her beloved nest,

All of that would be a luxury,

But on that table sat her teddy,

In his arms, she didn't have to play a 'lady',

They mocked her, called her a kid,

But little did they know,

That's where her home hid…

Your book

I opened your book one day, and wanted to dive in,

Dive in to those yellowed pages,

Into the peaceful solitude engraved in those Helvetica fonts.

I'd swim amidst the subplots and search that character,

Search that village boy with the freckled face,

Hair kissed by the sun.

I'd search him and ask him what it took,

What it took to make you fall,

What it took until you gave your all,

I'd get my answer, but I'll never really know,

So in his heart I'll live,

In your book I'll grow…

I'll then know why you love your books,

Nestled away in a valley,

I'll fall in love with you again,

You'll read me everyday,

Probably even then you'll not know,

The fragrance you'll find in those pages,

Was always yours to adore…

Drops

A gentle wring of his shirt,

A few drops of that shape-shifting liquid they called the rain.

But today it meant much more, the rain,

It wasn't just what wetted his hair everyday on his way home,

It wasn't just what formed those puddles on that street,

It wasn't just what flooded his spectacles,

Today was different.

Today was the first time that boy who hated the rain,

Had felt blessed in its presence...

Today was the first time he had held her hands,

As she was busy being her untamed self.

Today was the first time they danced with those drops,

Splashing, spraying, melting into a heavenly phenomenon.

A resplendent clash of two opposite souls,

And a promise of a love that would keep her close.

One that worshipped and the other that despised the rain,

And yet it was in that soulful face, amidst her hair unkempt,

He found those eyes that kept him sane,

A gentle sigh and a promise of an eternity,

To be witnesses to a lifetime of rain.

Jet Fumes

The amber skies of winter felt dead.

A cacophony of a few home bound birds,

The cutting cold of the northern breeze,

The barren mourning of skeletal trees,

All the elements were shaking him to the bone.

A tug at his taut heartstrings beckoned him to open up,

Opening up.

That seemed like a tall task these days.

While learning to hide, he must have forgotten how to show,

Or maybe revealing one's deepest feelings didn't always work out.

It sure didn't work out for him.

He wanted to be seen, he wanted to be heard,

Brighter than those jet fumes,

Louder than that lark.

In all those years of being lost,

He must have forgotten how to seek,

How to search for a connection in a smile,

Or cry out in anguish.

He watched that jet fly out instead,

Far away into the upper layers of the atmosphere,

He had read about in his science books.

The amber skies indeed felt dead from its roots...

Photograph

I still keep your photograph in my wallet.

A dusky beach for background,

An ice cream held up to your mouth in a pose,

With a smearing of white on your lips,

I wonder why I can't eat that flavour anymore.

Lychee used to be my favourite too.

Nights that take me back to those days,

And days that take me back to those nights,

Remind me of those little nuances that made you, you...

A sweet relief of your perfume every time we met,

Searched for a turmoil-stricken soul, and calmed it down,

Years later that soul sits on that beach,

Sand slipping out languidly through his fingers, like you did one day.

Tormented by the whims of a thousand emotions racing into my head,

Looking for that elusive release that lived in your smile gracing that picture.

I know your soft hands would never rest on my forehead again,

I know your warm embrace won't help me cope tonight.

But maybe, just maybe, a look at your messy photograph, as you savoured that ice cream,

Might calm me down,

As I wait for a tranquil dream to take me back to that garden we first met in,

Under the stars...

Keys

A troubled night awaited him. It's not that he didn't expect it.

As the rains beat down on his window pane,

The cold, damp floor reminded him of some other pain.

Another night, another season,

A delicate warmth by his side, and two minds devoid of reason.

As tangled blankets blended into the creases on that bedsheet,

He replayed her songs, as many as that record player would permit.

The warmth of the lamp was overwhelmed by the crisp night air,

As the bunch of keys swayed on the wall.

"Home, they say!"

A search for home within his home, that screamed vanity,

Or the horror in every note of those keys jingling,

Could she hear it as she flew miles up into that cloudy night sky?

Could she feel how cold his blanket was or how imperfect his tie?

Could she see those tiny little cars and mountains as well as she saw his heart?

The keys jingled deep into the night,

As his eyes craved for her sight...

Hold me

In the hollow of my hand, where the lines run,

In a reckless course of broken dreams and blunted ambition,

Or in mockery of an astrologer's prediction,

Hold me.

When the cold wind rummages through the filth I left behind,

And scatters away sheets of tainted paper,

Or freezes the red that wrote your name,

Hold me.

In the black of my hair, where insecurities live,

In a grotesquely haphazard mess of curls,

Or in a caress of calm,

Hold me.

When the light hurts the eye, and darkness soothes,

Or leaves me in a constant indecision of chasing one,

In a throbbing assault of optical flesh,

Hold me.

In the whisper of your name,

When you find a tinge of breathlessness,

Of a desperate age seeking solace,

Hold me.

May what we have ever had hold in a hug,

And may that hug hold,

Until I'm dead and cold.